Intruder

A Horrifying, Poetic Tale

M.L. McAmis

ARPress
45 Dan Road Suite 5
Canton MA 02021

Hotline: 1(888) 821-0229
Fax: 1(508) 545-7580

Ordering Information:

Quantity sales. Special discounts are available on quantity purchases by corporations, associations, and others. For details, contact the publisher at the address above.

Printed in the United States of America.

ISBN-13:   Softcover   979-8-89389-799-9
             eBook   979-8-89389-800-2

Library of Congress Control Number: 2024923344

I heard a noise, I know I did
In the other room, as if something big
There all alone, my fear came over me
Was it an intruder, a ghost, oh God, please help me

Slipped out of my bed, my cane I grabbed tight
My glasses, oh my I couldn't find, there was little light
Oh my, getting closer, I heard it in the hall
Felt for something, the door, the bed, the wall

Thank you Lord, there was the closet door
Slipped in quietly, I heard it on the nearby floor
Trembled then, feared for my life
Oh my, what if they had a gun, or a knife

Crashing sounds, pushed on my bed as well
I couldn't see much, but imagined it had a tail
Years of witchcraft, never anything like that
I wondered if my punishment was at hand, maybe tonight

A fierce growl, I could tell it was very large
That thing had definitely come in, and was taking charge
God please help, I'm sorry for my wrong doings, please
I was almost out of time, this thing was not there to tease

At the door, sniffing, I could hear and smell it's stench
Grabbing a handle, thank God, I found a wrench
Cane in one hand, wrench grasped in the other
The door came open, swinging, hitting, fighting, oh what a struggle

On the floor, it hit so hard, on it I was, somehow
Beating, taking charge, I was so proud
Moving no more, this thing I had killed
Come in on me no more, no longer free willed

To my feet, exhausted, leaned on my cane
I couldn't see much, maybe it had fangs
Reached for my glasses, I wanted to inspect
Now it was dead, by my hands, so what the heck

Oh yes, there they were, putting them on, still trembling
Goodness at all the blood, it covered everything
I saw a lump, in the middle of the rug
Now, oh my, to clean this off me, almost like on a drug

To the bathroom slowly I went, on my cane for support
Then set my bath, this mission I couldn't abort
A trash bag for those bloody clothes
Tied it tightly, sat aside, slipped to my bath, smelled of a rose

Scrubbed, splashed, soaked, oh so much blood
Reached for a towel, clean I stood
Glasses on then, lights and all, I could see
Back to the bedroom, oh again, couldn't find the light
I knew it was there, maybe a little to the right

I wanted to know what this was I had overcome
Wanted to clean that mess, a lot of things I am, but not dumb
There it was, gently put my finger on the lights witch
Thought, I will bury it, maybe in a ditch

On came the light, then focused my eyes to see
So bright, almost squinted, the darkness did flee
I saw it, I walked closer, lying still, it didn't move at all
First with my cane, walked slowly to see
It was, almost, oh my goodness, oh bad me

How could I, oh God please, oh I had done this
What could I do, who could help, a crime it was
Why did he not knock, why not talk to me
I thought he was a vamp, a ghost, or a demon to make flee

Another noise, oh my, they, he, the immortals smelled the blood
I had always went against them, in every way, and there they stood
We have never intervened, he said to me, never had a cause
You have slain an innocent, and now punishable, by our laws

On the floor laid my brother, I had killed in cold blood
Now facing the head immortals, my, all in black, there they stood
You threw your black magic at all, he said to me as he smiled
Even at us, and we never harmed you,even when running wild

All the while, me and mine sat by, waited for a flaw
After all these years, old man, you will pay, by our law
Take him, drink his blood, you can feast on him
I am old, I will stop my craft, please, as the light grew dim

Off my feet, his hand on my neck, I dropped my cane
Pulling me closer, looking in my eyes, his anger, his fangs
You detest me, you are more despicable than I thought
Slay your brother, offer him to us, against everything taught
Years of mischief, black magic, against us, and now you are caught

I have wealth, this I know interests you
Yes it does, although you could sing prison blues
Anything you want, name the price, land, anything
To my feet I was set, I saw retracting fangs

Follow me, to the next room we went
He named his price for a cover up, and he said help would be sent
I wrote a check, he snarled, tearing it up and threw it on the floor
Lead me to the safe, your money I have, then you go out the door

Much cash I handed him, into his trench it went
My rules, my way, he made blunt, go back to bed
There I went, covered my head, asleep in a bit
Morning came, on the edge of my bed I sat

Nothing, no body, no blood, nothing, not a shred of evidence
A few days passed, as I prayed, and some magic once more
Knock, knock, ring, oh my, who was at the door
Walked with my cane, I looked through the hole
Two officers, oh my God, I can't be on death row

Opened the door, friendly I was, offering some tea
Both officers agreed, none for me
Have you seen your brother, he's been gone for days
Quickly thought, answered no, not at all, his eyebrow raised

That is strange, as he wrote on his pad, he was seen here
Your neighbor saw him, a few days ago, I trembled with fear
Not knowing what to say, searching for words, what do I do
Thought of the vamps, the deal, but me, what will they do, sue

I am afraid officer, I do not want to tell
He was here, I remember it well
We talked, as usual over a cup of herbal tea
Then, a man dressed in black was standing in front of me

I am old, my brother is as well, looking at him, I saw his eyes
He must have picked my lock, to rob me, you know some will try
He took money from my safe, I will show you, come here
A beautiful lie, so great, I was loosing my fear

Opening the safe, I showed, I lied, I was covering
He believed me, he wrote it down, the lies, everything
Where is your brother, he asked, was he taken away
Oh yes, there were more than one, it was about mid day

Thinking maybe some of the evidence was still in my room
Some things are not swept away by a broom
The description I gave, I know that immortal well
He can be very malicious, I'd rather fight with hell

If behind bars, he could not harm me, thinking mischief
They took my brother away, then threatened me, that thief
I hope he is ok, I have worried for so long, many days
We will start looking, for both men, depending what the captain says

Out the door, I watched them drive away as I smiled
Knowing my guilt, much guilt for years, knowing all the while
Now remembering, what the immortal said to me
You have no recollection, no knowledge, do you see

A cover up, they did well, but a cover up, I do well
Like he said, I have battered all for years
No guilt, I only care for me, black magic
I cast, and have cast many viscous spells, would make you sick

To hell with all, my life is about my wealth
I don't care anything about anyone, much less their health
Night came, off to bed I went, no guilt, no remorse
Boom, my window, crack at the wall, many footsteps on my floors

Oh my God, a bag, a big bag he has, carried in his arms
The trash bag also, with the bloody clothes, in my head, many alarms
You will pay now, he snarled and threw the bags to the floor
A malicious vamp, he jerked me to my feet, what was in store

He shoved my head in the bag, I puked at the thought and smell
See what you did, you evil, old bastard, as he picked me up
I couldn't be found idiot, I am immortal, now, you I will dump
But, but, I will give more money, I have a lot, please
No, not interested, you broke our deal, we don't tease

Black you want, power you searched, power you've got
Look at me, as he yanked my hair, he smacked my face a lot
Thrown against the wall, I am old, so old
Your ass is mine, because your soul was sold

Lucifer is on my side, I yelled at the immortal
Laughing, he said, yep, now this kind of result he didn't tell
I started praying to God, please I am sorry, never again
The immortal snarled, you evil bastard, pay for your sins

I will bid all of my magic for you, please spare me now
Stopping his pursuit, interested a bit, I could tell he wondered how
Bruised and battered, to my feet I was then helped a bit
You bid for me, that is interesting, on my bed he then sat

I can give you spells, you had no clue did exist
Spells that repel almost all of harm, never again bothered by the rest
Just look at me, in my elderly age, never bothered by anyone
Always done things for me, built my wealth, questioned by none

I knew always, I could never make mistakes
For I would be attacked by you, the immortals, for goodness sakes
I have read many vamp books, true and false as well
I know there are good immortals and bad ones as well

I made several of my own spells, in that you are correct
Geared toward the immortals, I always tried to perfect
I know the vamps were the only ones to slow me down at all
For this reason, I cast spells to keep you away, so I couldn't fall

I can bid you in, a spell I have in mind for you
To you I will bid from this day forth, immortal all the way through
Always wondering, waiting for a day or night like this
Immortal I have always been, just a spell away, and there it was

He stood and looked down on my pleading face, serious, no smile
You have only one chance, prove yourself to me, for only a while
I stood on my feet, my glasses placed to my face
My cane in my hand, still in this race

Opened my personal journal, the perfect spell in hand
To make me the head immortal, over this land
You see, I always knew, a day like this might be
That is why I came up with this spell, to profit me

I went through the list of things I would need
I felt my heart darken, filling with greed
His head vampress, beautiful she was, as well
She, coming closer, as she would get my herbs for me, I could tell

Leaning to him, the head vamp in her ear, a whisper
Not hearing good, lost with my age, what did he tell her
Getting the list, he sent a few with her, for safety
They work this way, protecting one another, this I did see
This spell I have, years in the making, they will work for me

A short while passed, my herbs I did have
Little time to think, my spell book I did grab
All standing, except for the bloody corpse on the floor
I chanted the words, please gather gods, from shore to shore

Without hesitation, I saw the head immortal slowly turn away
What was he doing, he was doing something, but not going away
The herbs I mixed, in my bowl at this time
To hell with all, I will cover up this crime

What was that, no it cannot be, my brother moving behind me
I heard something else, the vamp, he, I cannot see
I turned, looked, what, I still did not see
No time to waste, I chanted the rest of the spell
The wind grew stronger, as if sent from hell

Dropped my cane, what just came over thee
Stood strong, yes, it worked, just for me
I heard it again, the body bag, it couldn't be
Turned to see, moving, ripping, open, is he mad at me

How, this was not done, he is dead, I did it myself
By his written will, I will get his wealth
The immortals too, where are they, they were here
Oh my God, he is going to get out of the body bag, oh my fear

The head vamp, that bastard must have done this
What was happening, I was changing, oh the pain, how fierce it was
Angry, gritting my teeth, and in pain, but it was going away
My glasses I threw to the wall, they shattered, on the floor they lay

Climbed to his feet, my brother I am sorry, do not harm
But, it is impossible, no marks, no blood, imagine my alarm
Smiling, he was happy, oh yes, my loving brother, come
But a hug was not in mind, I could tell, where is he, where from

In another world, in another life, in Heaven or hell
Why is he back, and no scratches, no blood at all
Walking to me, his lips slowly separating, his bottom teeth did fall
Opened his mouth, oh yes, I remember the spell I cast
This crime went away, my brother alive, it was over at last

Not to talk, not talking at all, though, open, so strange
Oh God, please help me, no, no, he has the most hideous fangs
Came closer, my fear, my strength grew all the while
Battle him again, I knew I would win, slam him on the hard tile

You stop now, I told him at least three times, maybe more
Never expecting this, my brother, he was lifeless on the floor
Then I knew, the battle never ends, I am immortal now
This was a battle to overcome, I must kill him, but how

Grabbed me, I swung at his head
I struck him violently, I smiled as he bled
Against the wall, we struggled for a bit
I went to the floor, so hard, so solid, my face was hit

His knee, I can cripple him, for my cane I did reach
I must crawl, while he was stomping my ribs, a lesson I'll teach
Grasping my cane, he tried to take it away
Kicked his neck, hit him frequently, on the floor he lay

To my feet I quickly rose, my cane high in the air
Cracked it against his knees, oh the blood, and that cold stare
He grabbed my cane, jerked it away, a hard lick to me with it
On the bed, I was knocked into a deep sleep
I remembered, the immortal I saw, had he come to reap

He said to me, you betrayed, and personally attacked me
I remember the eerie laugh, as he hovered, and then he did flee
Morning, I awoke, by a loud beating, who is at my door
To my feet, oh the energy I can feel well, what has today in store

My slippers on my feet, I went to the door
Mind racing, thoughts pumping, of the night before
Knocked louder, I am coming I screamed, my door open then
What, how, no, this cannot be, I covered it all, all of this sin

A blood soaked carpet, and the brutal, beaten corpse on the floor
The knocking, the corpse, the blood, I can make it no more
Yelling now, let us in, I cannot, whatever will I do
Running to my room, slamming the door, what now, no clue

We heard you sir, the voice still at the door, are you ok
Will they come in, will they go away, and me, where will I stay
The closet again, inside I will go, hide from this for a while
Kneeling to the keyhole, I can see all of the room, even the tile

My window, now knocking, they know I am here
Oh the guilt now, so remorseful, such agonizing fear
Yelling again, sir are you ok, never a sound, thinking go away
We are coming in, he shouted, they were there to stay

A hard thump, again and again, breaking it down
Safe I am, here in darkness, can I be found
Oh my, oh Lord in Heaven, I heard, on the radio he is now
Back up and ambulance, oh my, what will I do, what will they allow

He is dead, he said on the mike, we know who it is as well
Punished I should be, for years of no guilt, but please not jail
Through the house, combing, looking for me, I heard him say
Clean up this mess, leave me be, just go away

In my room, I saw him, through the hole
What kind of person would do this, they are so old
Then my thoughts, a grim look to me, my alibi
This looks like how I explained, for this I will surely fry

Closer to the door, his gun in his hand, now is open a bit
Are you ok, he asked, I acted terrified, as on the floor I did sit
I am so afraid, so afraid, I said, help me, is my brother ok
No sir, as he looked sad, he was murdered, away he was took

We have some questions, when you are ok of course, he said
Out of the closet, to the front room, I was then led
I was thinking, not talking at all, planning a story for them
I will tell now, what I saw, I stumbled forward, and spit my flem

They brought him back last night around twelve or one
The man threatened us both, hit my brother, as if for fun
I offered money, he said not tonight, he came to kill
They hit me a few times, dead I presume, to the old and ill

Then killing my brother, I saw it all, and warnings to me
Never tell what you saw, they said, and with that they did flee
I went quickly, to my room, needing an escape at the time
To my closet, I ran was all I could do, my closet, all mine

Writing quickly, the officer could hardly get down all my words
Flipping a page, slow down a bit he said, these I knew, pathetic nerds
Do you have a description, did you see faces, have any names at all
Yes sir, I do have descriptions, the leader for sure, very tall

His hair black and flowed long around his back as he moved
His face was mostly turned, like a mask never removed
I had no names, they didn't say them, I listened
Although his eyes, piercing at my soul, greenish blue and glistened

That was all I could see, and this while hitting at me
Was there more than one, how many did you see
At least four, maybe more, I am not sure, so chaotic
They believed every word, oh how gullible, how idiotic

I was told, we can put you in a safe place tonight
I am ok, just please send an officer to park out front until daylight
This we will do, he will be here after while, until tomorrow
You will be safe, we promise, we can't believe people can be so low

You just sit tight for a bit, we will get them all
Thinking greedily, all mine now, no more immortal, bye Mr. Tall
As the day passed on, I thought how great I felt inside
I was not feeling guilt, no remorse to the astral plane, indeed a ride

As darkness came, I made my way to bed, a little magic before sleep
So to travel, when in my bed asleep, I soar, with the best, a leap
I remember closing my eyes, there he was, oh, and with vengeance
What now, what now immortal, what now genius

I have done it, I now control you and all, head of the domain
Cast the spell, got away and an innocent I did kill, now I reign
Not a word, silence, eerie he always is, I hate, and respect him
What here, what will you do here, as the light went dim

A part of the astral plane, I had not been this far before
Wondering, watching, waiting, what could possibly be in store
Getting darker, almost totally dark, I heard he works this way
He works best in darkness, he roams silent, in search of prey

Where is he, I hear voices, not his, where are they
Reaching out my arms, feeling nothing, louder they, they
My ears, covering my ears, they know me, screaming my name
I cannot take this, all of this, any of this, did not want this fame

Touching me now, not harming, but annoying they are
Get away, flee all of you, agonizing voices, even from afar
I need to wake up, this will work, concentrate, wake
Eerie, loud, the touching, stop, all of you, for goodness sake

How do I leave, the darkness, I need to wake up, but how
Turning, only the same, screaming, oh God, so very, very loud
What do you want, who are you, what from me, what, what
Nothing but chants, my name against everything taught

At last, thank God, my eyes open, I see light, oh yes
Morning, feeling myself, no voices now, was that, maybe a test
The day went along, thinking tonight will be different I know
Same as the night before, ritual, sleep, then astral travel, away I go

What, why, here is the vamp again, still no words, and the darkness
The chants, my name I don't want to hear, oh the stress
Night after night, sequence was the same, never ending
Is this punishment, staying in my mind they are, for all my sinning

I did not sleep, for I knew what was in store
The voices, the touching, never again, to my bedroom door
Coffee I drank, up at night, always, I did stay
A while, this went on, but the immortals, they fixed new ways to play

In the lounge, on my sofa, I slept only under the sun
Although the voices still, the touching, oh they were having fun
Casting spell after spell, creating some, some against others
None worked, this I asked for, I have now, none seem like brothers

I saw the leader, the head vamp at first asleep, each, every time
To him I began to ask questions, are you punishing me for my crime
Never talking, only making his presence known, he did this so well
This has to be it, a test, to see if I go to Heaven, or rot in Hell

Made my mind, tonight again I will not sleep, immortal I am
The darkness came, the voices, the touching, damn now, damn
Seized for a bit, became very calm, no touching, no chants
Footsteps, a dim light, in the distance, a dark cloak, I got a glance

Neared quickly, it was, I thought, maybe a lantern I could see
It was cloaked, a sound, what was that, the Reaper coming for me
I stood my ground, as if to rule over him, go away, leave
But closer, and the sound, I heard a chain, amongst his sleeve

You have no cycle, laughing, you are weak, leave me now, shew
He, hearing as I spoke, his face under his cloak, get what is due
That was his words, what is due, you get away with that chain
But raised it, placing it around me, I almost preferred being slain

Still no face, only the stench, and such stench he had
I could not break free, tightened on my ankle, then gave a nod
My waist, my ankles, chained, I could not run, only my arms free
Locks he placed, where the chains came together, then to an oak tree

This all in an instant, although I remember it all, in detail
The Reaper chained me, leaving my arms free, my hands as well
Every night, as sleep I went, the tree, chained, every night
Not free to roam the astral plane, not free at all, the chains so tight

My arms and hands, they were free, but why
Night after night, this repeating, oh please end, oh a spell I must try
Before bed, I did it, I remember, I cast, oh yes, the perfect spell
It was geared at the head vamp, to summons him, what the hell

As quickly as asleep, the chains I did feel once more, but, but then
Out of the darkness, oh yes, it worked, where have you been
Not talking, speak to me I shouted, as he looked down on me
You bastard, I said, you did this, your face, I can read, I can see

No words, you speak, you tell what I need to know, swinging at him
But, behind him, there they came again, the light was so dim
My spell book, you damn vampress, give that to me
Reached, swung, oh you will pay, but I couldn't run, that damn tree

My altar, put that down now, now I screamed, put it down
The screams, the cursing, the swinging, no, not even a small affect
They gathered, but why, so many of them, what to bite my neck
Maybe spells, my spells to cast for them, oh maybe indeed
That must be it, I cast spells for them, oh they must be in need

But, my book, she was not bringing it to me, but why
And my altar, sitting out of my reach, bastards, I screamed to the sky
But what are you doing, I asked, he was still telling her something
Gather sticks, leaves, and logs, she said, for our chained king

An altar, oh yes, a bonfire just for me, I laughed aloud
They gathered it, in a short time, I screamed yes, make me proud
My altar, my sacred altar, was then placed near my knees
My spell book, brought to me, I said, open it please

But then, everything changed, oh the chants again
And the wood, both sides of me, placed on both sides of me then
My feet covered, but the chains, oh how tightly they were
Jerking, cursing, then he said, you address me as sir

Those, those were the first, the only words he ever said to me
I will never, I shouted, and spat at him, and tugged against the tree
The wood quickly piling, my waist it was to then, still piling atop
But my arms were free, I fought, they would not stop

The head vamp, he walked away, into the night, but returned in a bit
He carried an unlit torch, oh please God I screamed, please not lit
The words had hardly come out when, oh my goodness, and nearing
Getting his revenge, his face said it all, I was hearing

Touching the torch to the altar, oh the heat, and the flames
The flames covered me, oh how I screamed, as if no shame
I remembered it well, he walking away, never coming back
Every night, I burned when asleep, and still do, every night
I burn I tell you, every time there is absence of light

I still have my days, oh hell yes, I still have my days, though
I feel so young, immortal, a day vamp that escaped death row
At night I pay, I pay for my evil, but under the sun, under it I reign
This is how I feed, in broad daylight, I find one, I sink my fangs